WHO IS CHRIST?

WHO IS CHRIST?

Biblical Perspective on the Person of Jesus

Melody Wolfe

authorHOUSE®

AuthorHouse™
1663 Liberty Drive
Bloomington, IN 47403
www.authorhouse.com
Phone: 1 (800) 839-8640

Published by AuthorHouse 09/06/2016

ISBN: 978-1-5246-3872-6 (sc)
ISBN: 978-1-5246-3871-9 (e)

Print information available on the last page.

This book is printed on acid-free paper.

NIV
Scripture quotations marked NIV are taken from the Holy Bible, New
International Version®. NIV®. Copyright © 1973, 1978, 1984 by International
Bible Society. Used by permission of Zondervan. All rights reserved. [Biblica]

TABLE OF CONTENTS

DEDICATION

This book is dedicated with much love and affection to my
Lord and Savior, Jesus Christ. No human author could give
Your Precious Name the glory that it deserves. I believe with
all my heart that You will touch people's lives through this
book, and I give You all the glory! I love You, my Lord.

ACKNOWLEDGMENTS

Hannah Wolfe – You are such a blessing to me. I am so very proud to be your mom. You're growing into a lovely young lady. I pray that the Lord would grant you the desires of your heart. I love you!

Lydia Wolfe – You're my little ray of sunshine! Every day you make me proud to be your mother. You're my gift from God. May you grow in the grace and knowledge of our Lord and Savior, Jesus Christ.

Susan Hogg – Thank you for always being there and for loving me during those times when many would have suggested that I was unlovable. You're a fantastic mom, and I'm so thankful to God for you. May blessings from above be poured into your life in abundance!

Dana Hogg – Thank you for being such a wonderful father. Thank you for all that you do for your family. You are a rare and precious jewel, and I know that you will receive a rich welcome into the Kingdom of God one day. May God strengthen your frame and prolong your days. I love you.

Debbie Grandy – You are more than an aunt to me; you are my beloved sister. Thank you for your continued kindness to me. I love you very much.

Michelle Marriott – You are such a wonderful friend. We go back together so many years, and I praise God for our friendship. Thank you for your words of hope and encouragement. May God bless you and your family, my friend.

A PRELUDE

Jesus Christ – how does one begin to describe Him with words? He is love, eternal and is the one we must come to for salvation. Despite all the running from Him that we can do, there will come a day when we will have to stop running and face Him. We will either face Him as Savior, or as Judge.

Since the time that Jesus walked the earth over 2,000 years ago, many have wondered who this Jesus really is. In Matthew 16:13-17 we read: *When Jesus came to the region of Caesarea Philippi, he asked his disciples, "Who do people say the Son of Man is?" They replied, "Some say John the Baptist; others say Elijah; and still others, Jeremiah or one of the prophets." "But what about you?" he asked. "Who do you say I am?" Simon Peter answered, "You are the Christ, the Son of the living God." Jesus replied, "Blessed are you Simon son of Jonah, for this was not revealed to you by man, but by my Father in heaven. And I tell you that you are Peter, and on this rock I will build my church, and the gates of Hades will not overcome it."*

What a great gift that Peter had from the Father! He received revelation knowledge from God concerning Jesus, and Peter believed. The Holy Spirit is at work with people who do not know Jesus personally. He is preparing their hearts to receive the Messiah, who is Jesus. Sadly, many people, for whatever the reason, dismiss the Holy Spirit's wooing and do not receive Christ as their Savior, Lord and friend. This is the worst tragedy possible.

This book is going to demonstrate to you, from Scripture, that Jesus is who He claimed to be. Jesus was not merely a good person or a kind man. He is the Creator of the world, and He created you and me to have a deeply fulfilling relationship with Him. He is not far off and distant; rather, He lives on the inside of everyone who puts their faith and trust in Him for salvation. One could study Jesus an entire life-time and still not fully grasp the awesomeness of God. And that is who Jesus is – He is God in the flesh.

One of the issues that we need to examine is the character of Christ. Just who is He? What is He passionate about? Will He come through for me and help me? Does He really want me to be part of His Kingdom? If we only could grasp, even for a second, the awesome love that Christ has for every one of us, we would never be the same. When I consider just how often I fall short of His glory, and when I consider how many times He has welcomed me back, I am moved in spirit. What a tender and loving Shepherd this Jesus is!

Sadly, in today's culture, His precious name is used in profanity or in course joking. Acts 4:12 says, *Salvation is found in no one else, for there is no other name under heaven given to men by which we must be saved.* The world teaches there are many ways to heaven – many paths to "enlightenment." This is not what the Bible teaches. John 14:6 says, *Jesus answered, "I am the way and the truth and the life. No one comes to the Father except through me."* What a statement! His words here should not be ignored or dismissed, but given full recognition. If Jesus is the only way to the Father, then it is vitally important that we know Jesus personally. One can know about someone, but that does not necessarily mean that they know this person intimately. No other relationship is as important as our relationship with Christ. When all has been said and done, our eternal destiny is summed up with this one question: Do you know Jesus? If you do, then I pray this book brings you into a deeper understanding of your God and Savior. If you have not yet received Jesus as your Lord, then my prayer for you is that God will use this book to demonstrate your need for Christ.

Jeremiah 15:16 When your words came, I ate them; they were my joy and my heart's delight, for I bear your name, O Lord God Almighty.

CHAPTER 1

JESUS – YOUR CREATOR

It is so marvelous to me that I was created by Jesus and for Jesus. I did not come from an ape, nor was I a result from some big bang in the universe. I was created by a Divine designer, and He knows how to complete the work He has created. Before the world was ever created, Jesus knew all about me – and He planned for my existence! Colossians 1:15-17 says, *He is the image of the invisible God, the firstborn over all creation. For by him all things were created: things in heaven and on earth, visible and invisible, whether thrones or powers or rulers or authorities; all things were created by him and for him. He is before all things, and in him all things hold together.*

It is sad to see how the world has dismissed this dynamic truth. We, as a society, have abandoned the reality of God's existence and His pre-eminence. Our children are not being taught about creation in schools any longer. It is vitally important for us as parents to present the truth about creation to our children. Both of my daughters go to a public school where they are taught the Big Bang Theory. I make every effort, along with my church, to teach them where they really come from and who created them. The knowledge that they were created for a purpose and not just by some cosmic accident, gives them a sense of value and worth.

When Jesus came to earth over 2,000 years ago, the world did not recognize or receive Him as their Creator. John 1:10-11 tells us this: *He was in the world, and though the world was made through him, the world did not recognize him. He came to that which was his own, but his own did not receive him.* In John 1:1-4 we read, *In the beginning was the Word, and the Word was with God, and the Word was God. He was with God in the beginning. Through him all things were made; without him nothing was made that has been made. In him was life, and that life was the light of men."* We see from these passages that Jesus, who is called the Word, created all things. Verse 1 tells us that not only had Jesus been with God before He came to earth, but that Jesus was God!

Now that we have established that Christ Jesus created all things, let's take a look at the creation of the first man and woman on earth – Adam and Eve. Let's pay particular attention to how they related with God before the fall of mankind. Let's look at Genesis 2:4-9: *This is the account of the heavens and the earth when they were created. When the Lord God made the earth and the heavens – and no shrub of the field had yet appeared on the earth and no plant of the field had yet sprung up, for the Lord God had not sent rain on the earth and there was no man to work the ground, but streams came up from the earth and watered the whole surface of the ground – the Lord God formed the man from the dust of the ground and breathed into his nostrils the breath of life, and the man became a living being. Now the Lord God had planted a garden in the east, in Eden; and there he put the man he had formed. And the Lord God made all kinds of trees grow out of the ground – trees that were pleasing to the eye and good for food. In the middle of the garden were the tree of life and the tree of the knowledge of good and evil.* Let's consider for a moment the beauty of how God created Adam – He breathed into his nostrils the breath of life. He breathes that same life into us today when we receive Christ into our hearts. After Christ rose from the dead, He breathed on His disciples and told them to receive the Holy Spirit. (John 20:22) His Spirit brings life to us and we are made alive in Christ upon salvation. Now let us continue on to see how God created the first woman.

Genesis 2:18-25 says, *The Lord God said, "It is not good for the man to be alone. I will make a helper suitable for him." Now the Lord God had formed out of the ground all the beasts of the field and all the birds of the air. He brought them to the man to see what he would name them; and whatever the man called each living creature, that was its name. So the man gave names to all the livestock, the birds of the air and all the beasts of the field. But for Adam no suitable helper was found. So the Lord God caused the man to fall into a deep sleep; and while he was sleeping, he took one of the man's ribs and closed up the place with flesh. Then the Lord God made a woman from the rib he had taken out of the man, and he brought her to the man. The man said, "This is now bone of my bones and flesh of my flesh; she shall be called 'woman,' for she was taken out of man." For this reason a man will leave his father and mother and be united to his wife, and they will become one flesh. The man and his wife were both naked, and they felt no shame.*

There was no sin in the world when Adam and Eve were first created. They enjoyed complete fellowship with one another but, even more amazing than that, they enjoyed a beautiful relationship with God Himself! God would walk in the garden in the cool of the day, and He enjoyed His creation very much. At some point, however, the devil, in the form of a serpent, deceived Eve into disobeying God's command to not eat from the tree of the knowledge of good and evil. Eve ate the fruit and then gave some of it to her husband, and he ate of it too. You may read about this account in Genesis chapter 3. Because of this single act of disobedience, sin entered the world and was passed on to every human being who has ever lived, with the exception of Jesus. After they had eaten the fruit, they heard God walking in the garden and they hid themselves because they were ashamed. In Genesis 3:9 we read, *But the Lord God called to the man, "Where are you?"* I believe that God still calls the lost with those same words – where are you? If you are anywhere other than in God's grace through Jesus Christ, then you are lost. There is hope, though! Jesus came to seek and save that which was lost. We will study that point in greater detail later on in this book.

We see now how God created Adam and Eve, but how did he create you and me? Psalm 13913-16 tells us this: *For you created my inmost being; you knit me together in my mother's womb. I praise you because I am fearfully and wonderfully made; your works are wonderful, I know that full well. My frame was not hidden from you when I was made in the secret place. When I was woven together in the depths of the earth, your eyes saw my unformed body. All the days ordained for me were written in your book before one of them came to be.* How precious we are to God! He absolutely loves His creation. He has a plan for every one of us that is so beautiful. Be blessed to know that you were not a mistake – God Almighty planned your existence from the foundation of the world, and He loves you!

If I were to build, let's say, a coffee maker – I would be the one who knew best how it worked and what it needed to keep functioning. It is the same with Jesus. He created us and, therefore, He knows best what we need to function properly in this world. He knows what would be in our best interest more than we ourselves know. Jesus does not intend for us to run our own lives; rather, He is the One to Whom we should submit to and trust in for guidance and direction. We like to believe that we have it all under control and that our plan is right. Should we not, at the very least, consult with Jesus about the direction He wants our lives to go in? True wisdom is saying to Christ, "Lord, my life belongs to You. You created me for a purpose. How would You like me to proceed? Where would You like me to go? Direct my steps and order my days, for to You, my Creator, I lift up my soul!" If we all prayed like that, the chaos would vanish and perfect order and unity would be established. A heart that is surrendered to Jesus is a heart that is filled with peace. Open your heart to your Creator today!

NOTES AND REFLECTIONS

NOTES AND REFLECTIONS

NOTES AND REFLECTIONS

CHAPTER 2

JESUS – THE SON OF GOD

As humans, we are used to a beginning and an end of something. The thought of someone being eternal is staggering. This, however, is what God is – eternal. Christ's life did not begin in a stable on Christmas morning; He existed before time began. When John the Baptist was speaking about Jesus, he described Him this way in John 1:30: *This is the one I meant when I said, 'A man who comes after me has surpassed me because he was before me.'* John the Baptist was older than Jesus in the flesh, but he knew that Christ was eternal and existed before he was ever born. Jesus is the living Son of God.

When Jesus lived on the earth, He represented the exact being of His Father. Jesus said in John 10:30 the following: *I and the Father are one.* Even Jesus' disciples did not fully recognize this point. In John 14:7-11, Jesus says, *"If you really knew me, you would know my Father as well. From now on, you do know him and have seen him." Philip said, "Lord, show us the Father and that will be enough for us." Jesus answered, "Don't you know me, Philip, even after I have been among you such a long time? Anyone who has seen me has seen the Father. How can you say, 'Show us the Father'? Don't you believe that I am in the Father, and that the Father is in me? The words I say to you are not just my own. Rather, it is the Father, living in me, who is doing his work. Believe me when I say that I am in the Father and the Father is in me; or at least believe on the evidence of the miracles themselves."* Jesus represents the heart of our heavenly Father. God sent His Son into the world to be its Savior. Jesus is the way to the Father – the only way. John

14:6 says, *Jesus answered, "I am the way and the truth and the life. No one comes to the Father except through me."*

Jesus existed in glory with the Father before time began. When praying to His Father in John 17:5, Jesus said, *"And now, Father, glorify me in your presence with the glory I had with you before the world began."* The question one may ask is this: What prompted Jesus to leave His Father and come to earth? The answer is found in John 3:16-17: *For God so loved the world that he gave his one and only Son, that whoever believes in him shall not perish but have eternal life. For God did not send his Son into the world to condemn the world, but to save the world through him.* This proves that Scripture is correct when it tells us that God is love. (1 John 4:8) Imagine, for a moment, just how much God loves His Son Jesus. Then imagine how much God loves us to send His one and only Son to the earth to pay the penalty for our sins. I have children, and the thought of this kind of love is over-whelming. Jesus, like His Father, demonstrated His own love for us when He laid down His life for our Salvation. Jesus said to His disciples in John 15:13 this: *Greater love has no one than this, that he lay down his life for his friends.*

Jesus is the King of kings and Lord of lords; yet, He was willing to humble Himself to the point of death on the cross out of His love for us. No greater sacrifice has ever been offered in all of eternity. The humility of the Son of God is seen at work shortly before His arrest and crucifixion. At the last supper, Jesus washed His disciples' feet. (John 13:1-17) The Son of God came to earth as a servant, and He has left us with a wonderful example to follow. The heart of God is that of a servant. Philippians 2:5-11 gives us great insight into the character of the Son of God: *Your attitude should be the same as that of Christ Jesus: Who, being in very nature God, did not consider equality with God something to be grasped, but made himself nothing, taking the very nature of a servant, being made in human likeness. And being found in appearance as a man, he humbled himself and became obedient to death – even death on a cross! Therefore God exalted him to the highest place and gave him the name that is above every name, that at the name of Jesus every knee should bow, in heaven and on earth and under the earth, and every tongue confess that Jesus Christ is Lord, to the glory of God the Father.*

Jesus, the Son of God, has transformed my life. He has called me to His side and has given me a great desire to know Him. He is willing to do the same for you. You may be reading this book and wondering, "How does all of this apply to me?" The Son of God gave His life on the cross for you, that you might spend eternity with Him. He has a beautiful plan for your life that will resound in all of eternity. There is no greater invitation – no higher purpose or calling than what God has for you. Jesus knows everything about you and loves you. Even when I am in the wrong, Jesus is always ready to forgive me and bestow His favor upon me. Knowing that the Son of God wants me for His very own gives me a sense of worth and value.

Jesus is the Son of God, as well as God, from all eternity. When He entered the world in the flesh, He was born of a virgin, conceived by the Holy Spirit. After His resurrection, He was glorified and is now seated at the right hand of God the Father. As mentioned before, the only way to the Father is through the Son. If you do not know the Son of God as your personal Lord and Savior, then I ask you to not put this off any longer. Your eternal destiny is at stake with this one decision: Will you receive Jesus, the Son of God, into your heart? My prayer for you is that you will.

NOTES AND REFLECTIONS

NOTES AND REFLECTIONS

NOTES AND REFLECTIONS

CHAPTER 3

JESUS – GOD IN THE FLESH

The reality that Jesus has a body that is now glorified is a great and beautiful mystery to me. Jesus declared in John 4:24 this: *God is spirit, and his worshippers must worship in spirit and in truth.* He was speaking of God the Father, who is in fact a spirit-being. Jesus was a spirit-being before He came to earth. Hebrews 10:5-7 says, *Therefore, when Christ came into the world, he said: "Sacrifice and offering you did not desire, but a body you prepared for me; with burnt offerings and sin offerings you were not pleased. Then I said, 'Here I am – it is written about me in the scroll – I have come to do your will, O God.'"* God prepared a body for His Son because Jesus would have to have a physical body with blood. His blood was to be shed for the remission of sins. Hebrews 9:22 tells us this: *In fact, the law requires that nearly everything be cleansed with blood, and without the shedding of blood there is no forgiveness.* Under the law (the Old Covenant), animals were sacrificed to cover over sins. This was a shadow of what Christ would do once and for all by His own body – He shed His precious blood on the cross to take away sins. No further sacrifice is needed.

In a Bible study that I facilitate, a woman recently shared with me how she felt that God was being unfair in requiring Jesus, His Son, to die for sinners when He Himself had committed no sin. My response to that was that Jesus loved us enough to die for us, knowing full well that we could never have saved ourselves. This also demonstrates just how much our Heavenly Father loves us. Hebrews 12:2-3 is a beautiful answer to this lady's reasoning: *Let us fix our eyes on Jesus, the author and perfecter of our faith, **who for the joy set before him endured the cross,** scorning its* shame, and sat down at the right hand of the throne of God. *Consider him who endured such opposition from sinful men, so that you will not grow weary and lose heart.* This passage of Scripture brings great comfort to my soul, because as a person involved in ministry, I have encountered opposition before. Knowing that Jesus experienced that Himself and was victorious gives me great hope! There is nothing more important to me than sharing the plan of salvation with people. Sharing with others who Christ really is makes my heart rejoice.

We have established that Christ died on the cross, shedding His blood, for our sins. Let us look at what happened next. In the Gospels (Matthew, Mark, Luke and John), we discover that Jesus was buried in a tomb. This was a tomb in which no one had ever been buried. His disciples were stricken with grief because it seemed as though their hopes were shattered because Jesus had died. On the third day after His death, God raised Jesus to life again. He was raised with a glorified body. After His resurrection, in His glorified body, He could appear at will, defying the laws of physics. He could still eat and drink, and He could be touched. 1 John 1:1 says, *That which was from the beginning, which we have heard, which we have seen with our eyes, which we have looked at and our hands have touched – this we proclaim concerning the Word of life.* Individuals who receive Jesus as their Savior will one day have a glorified body like that of Christ's body. Philippians 3:20-21 promises us the following: *But our citizenship is in heaven. And we eagerly await a Savior from there, the Lord Jesus Christ, who, by the power that enables him to bring everything under his control, will transform our lowly bodies so that they will be like his glorious body.*

Isaiah prophesied centuries before the birth of Christ that Jesus would suffer and die for our sins. Let me share Isaiah chapter 53 with you: *Who has believed our message and to whom has the arm of the Lord been revealed? He grew up before him like a tender shoot, and like a root out of dry ground. He had no beauty or majesty to attract us to him, nothing in his appearance that we should desire him. He was despised and rejected by men, a man of sorrows, and familiar with suffering. Like one from whom men hide their faces he was despised, and we esteemed him not. Surely he took up our infirmities and carried our sorrows, yet we considered him stricken by God, smitten by him, and afflicted. But he was pierced for our transgressions, he was crushed for our iniquities; the punishment that brought us peace was upon him, **and by his wounds we are healed**. We all, like sheep, have gone astray, each of* *us has turned to his own way; and the Lord has laid on him the iniquity of us all. He was oppressed and afflicted, yet he did not open his mouth; he was led like a lamb to the slaughter, and as a sheep before her shearers is silent, so he did not open his mouth. By oppression and judgment he was taken away. And who can speak of his descendants? For he was cut off from the land of the living; for the transgression of my people he was stricken. He was assigned a grave with the wicked, and with the rich in his death, though he had done no violence, nor was any deceit in his mouth. Yet it was the Lord's will to crush him and cause him to suffer, and though the Lord makes his life a guilt offering, he will see his offspring and prolong his days, and the will of the Lord will prosper in his hand. After the suffering of his soul, he will see the light of life, and be satisfied; by his knowledge my righteous servant will justify many, and he will bear their iniquities. Therefore I will give him a portion among the great, and he will divide the spoils with the strong, because he poured out his life unto death, and was numbered with the transgressors. For he bore the sin of many, and made intercession for the transgressors.*

As previously mentioned, Isaiah prophesied concerning Christ centuries before Jesus came to earth. When reading the account of His death and resurrection in the Gospels, we see that this prophecy came true concerning Jesus. Consider the love of God – that He would love us so much to send His Son as a sacrifice for our sins! We did not deserve this kind of grace and mercy; we deserved eternal separation from God for all eternity. However, God in His grace provided us a way of escape that we may fellowship with Him once again, as Adam and Eve did in the Garden of Eden. One day, in the not too distant future, Jesus will return to earth to establish His Kingdom forever. (We will study this fact later on in another chapter.) Those whom have put their faith in Jesus for salvation will see Him as their Beloved Savior face to face, and we will spend eternity with Jesus – God in the flesh. I will close this chapter with this beautiful scripture in Romans 5:8: *But God demonstrates his own love for us in this: While we were still sinners, Christ died for us.*

NOTES AND REFLECTIONS

NOTES AND REFLECTIONS

NOTES AND REFLECTIONS

CHAPTER 4

JESUS – THE BELIEVER'S CLOSEST FRIEND

Throughout the course of my life, I have had the privilege of having many good friends. God has brought some amazing friendships into my life through my church, and it is a blessing to have these individuals in my life. However, there is no other friend dearer to me than Jesus. He's been my best friend since I gave my heart to Him when I was four, and He has never left me alone. Hebrews 13:5 says, *Keep your lives free from the love of money and be content with what you have, because God has said,* ***"Never will I leave you; never will I forsake you."*** I have come to learn that I can never run from the presence of God, nor can I do anything that will cause Him to go against His Word and leave me. I have been through many difficult "storms" throughout the years, and Jesus has always been there to comfort and heal me. He is closer to me than any other friend in my life.

In John 15:13-15, Jesus declared the following: *Greater love has no one than this, that he lay down his life for his friends. You are my friends if you do what I command. I no longer call you servants, because a servant does not know his master's business. Instead, I have called you friends, for everything that I learned from my Father I have made known to you.* What a wonderful expression of love – that God Himself would call me a friend!

I have one particular memory where I truly felt the Lord's Divine friendship. I was going through a particularly difficult time in my life, and I happened to be on the streets alone at night. I was nervous because I felt so lost and confused. I was in a very abusive relationship at the time, and I had just left this man's home and had to make my way back to the Second Stage Housing Project where I was living at the time. As I was waiting at the bus terminal to head home, I received revelation from God that Jesus was right there with me, walking me back home. I'll never forget that as long as I live. In my most desperate time of need, when I believed that God should have been very angry with me because of my lifestyle, He was there to restore me and protect me. This is friendship at its finest!

God truly cares about your circumstances and your life. He is deeply invested into your spirit, and He treasures you with a love that is unfathomable to the human mind. When others may fail you, or give up on you, Jesus is there to fill the void and take care of you. When we decide to dismiss His leading, we can find ourselves in some very dark and depressing places. But God has not placed us there – we have! Jesus is the tender Shepherd who leads us beside peaceful waters (see Psalm 23) and restores our soul. In society, many people "fall through the cracks" and find themselves in agonizing situations. Homelessness, prostitution, drug and alcohol abuse, starvation and a host of other tragedies leave people asking, "Where is God in any of this?" If we would look to Him for help, He will joyfully and tenderly lead us out of trouble into His safe and loving arms. Trials and sufferings are a part of life at times, but that does not change the fact that God is a good God. He is for you, not against you.

The amazing aspect of Jesus' friendship with the Believer is that there are no conditions to it. He is not our friend only during the times when we are good, but He is there to lead us back to Himself when our behavior is out of line with His Word. He has never once said to me, "Melody, you have gone too far this time. I am no longer willing to be your friend." Others have said that to me, but Jesus never has. I used to struggle with fear of abandonment, but after years of experiencing the love of Christ for myself, this fear has left me. Psalm 27:10 says, *Though my father and mother forsake me, the Lord will receive me.* If I were to lose every relationship and friendship that I have, I would still be okay because I have Jesus. He is more than enough! I enjoy the relationships that I have in my life, but I am not dependant upon them for my happiness; rather, I depend on Christ to meet my every need, even the need for companionship.

It would be silly to talk about friendship with Jesus without touching on the subject of prayer. Prayer is not some religious duty or obligation. It is fellowship with God Himself, and who wouldn't want to have access to the Author of Life? Prayer opens the door for us to pour out things on our hearts that we could not possibly share with anyone else. It also opens the door for the Lord to speak to our spirits and guide us. Talking with Jesus has become as natural to me as taking a breath of air into my lungs, and it is as vital to me as oxygen. I know that when I pray to my best friend (Jesus), He is listening and delighting in my relationship with Him. This is how intimacy with my Creator is developed and strengthened.

Studying the Word of God is just as important. It is through the Bible that we learn who Jesus really is, and who we are in Him. The world has many lies to offer us. It is only by being grounded in the truth of God's Word that we recognize reality from fantasy. The world has many enticements and holds out a deceptive hope of pleasure; but, it is only a fleeting pleasure that has no lasting value in our lives. James 4:4 warns us of the following: *You adulterous people, don't you know that friendship with the world is hatred toward God? Anyone who chooses to be a friend of the world becomes an enemy of God.*

When praying to His Father shortly before His crucifixion, Jesus prayed the following in John 17:14-19: *I have given them your word and the world has hated them, for they are not of the world any more than I am of the world. My prayer is not that you take them out of the world but that you protect them from the evil one. They are not of the world, even as I am not of it. Sanctify them by the truth; your word is truth. As you sent me into the world, I have sent them into the world. For them I sanctify myself, that they too may be truly sanctified.* The interests of the world are not the same interests of God. Jesus has your best interest at heart. The question is: Do you trust Him as your friend?

I do. I trust Him completely. Even when things do not go my way, I know that God is in control. I do not have to try and figure everything out in my own strength – I simply have to believe that God's Word is true and He's my friend. I have not always been such a good friend back to Jesus, though. I have been downright selfish and self-centered. But I'm learning by His example what it means to be a good friend. Jesus is my teacher, and there's nothing too difficult for Him. Allow Jesus to be your friend today. Invite Him into your heart and life. He desires to be involved with you so much. Whatever your circumstances may be, Jesus is the answer.

NOTES AND REFLECTIONS

NOTES AND REFLECTIONS

NOTES AND REFLECTIONS

CHAPTER 5

JESUS – THE CHRISTIAN'S ADVOCATE

When speaking of Christ as our advocate with the Father, the word simply means "defender." 1 John 2:1 states: *My dear children, I write this to you so that you will not sin. But if anybody does sin, we have one who speaks to the Father in our defense – Jesus Christ, the Righteous One.* This is a very comforting thought, in light of the fact that we all stumble and fall. None of us are perfect; we all have a sin nature. We should never use God's grace as an excuse to sin, but when we do sin, Jesus is there to defend us.

What is our defense? The blood of Christ! Jesus is in heaven, seated at the right hand of God, and He intercedes for us on our behalf. When God the Father sees us, he no longer sees our sin – He sees the righteousness of His Son that has been given to us through faith in His Name. Because I am all too familiar with my own weaknesses and struggles, I am forever grateful that Christ bridges the gap between mankind and God. The one who has rejected Jesus as their Savior does not have Christ as an Advocate. However, for the Believer, Jesus is always willing to defend us. Does He defend us based on our own righteousness? Absolutely not! He advocates for us based on His own righteousness that was imparted to us at the moment of salvation.

Satan is the great accuser. He accuses Christians night and day, but Jesus is there to plead our case before the throne of God. Revelation 12:7-12 says, *And there was war in heaven. Michael and his angels fought against the dragon, and the dragon and his angels fought back. But he was not strong* *enough, and they lost their place in heaven. The great dragon was hurled down – that ancient serpent called the devil, or Satan, who leads the whole world astray. He was hurled to the earth, and his angels with him. Then I heard a loud voice in heaven say: "Now have come the salvation and the power and the kingdom of our God, and the authority of his Christ. **For the accuser of our brothers, who accuses them before our God day and night, has been hurled down**. They overcame him by the blood of the Lamb and by the word of their testimony; they did not love their lives so much as to shrink from death. Therefore rejoice, you heavens and you who dwell in them! But woe to the earth and the sea, because the devil has gone down to you! He is filled with fury, because he knows that his time is short."*

Satan tempts the Christian to sin. If the Christian yields to that sin, Satan then becomes our accuser. There is hope in this situation, though. James 4:7 tells us this: *Submit yourselves, then, to God. Resist the devil, and he will flee from you.* Notice that our first admonition is to submit to God. This means that we determine to obey God in whatever situation we find ourselves in. Then, we are to resist the devil and he will flee from us. In Christ, we have the victory over sin. We do not have to yield to the temptations of our flesh or the temptations that the devil sends our way. Christ has already won the battle, for He defeated sin at the cross.

Let me share a human example from my own life to help illustrate this point. When I was 22, I found myself in conflict with the law and, as such, had to appear in court several times. I was guilty, and I was willing to acknowledge my guilt to the court and pray to God for mercy. I had a human advocate – a lawyer – who was a lovely lady who cared about women and mental illness. She advocated for me to receive a merciful sentence whereby I could receive treatment for my mental health disorder. Had it not been for the fact that she truly cared about my life, the outcome could have been so much worse. The court accepted her proposal and I received a rather lenient sentence, with a condition to receive treatment from a highly qualified professional. As good of an advocate that she was, though, Jesus is even greater! When He advocates for us, in God's Holy presence, the verdict of "not guilty based on the blood of Christ" is what Christians receive. And Jesus never grows weary of us! His forgiveness and mercy is supreme – we have passed from death to life!

When a person is not saved, they do not belong to Christ. However, the believer does belong to Jesus and, as such, is no longer free to live as the world lives. The struggle with ongoing sin in our lives is proof that we are in Christ, for if there was no struggle at all, we would be free to live as the world lives. But we have been called to a higher calling – one of obedience to Christ. Paul describes the Christian's struggle with sin in Romans 7:14-17: *We know that the law is spiritual, but I am unspiritual, sold as a slave to sin. I do not understand what I do. For what I want to do I do not do, but what I hate I do. And if I do what I do not want to do, I agree that the law is good. As it is, it is no longer I myself who do it, but it is sin living in me.* According to this passage, we see that while we are in the tent of this body, we are going to struggle with sin. However, Jesus Christ has won this battle for us and, as we abide in Him and He in us, we will begin to see victory in those areas of weakness. It is comforting to know that through the process of this journey, we have an Advocate – Jesus Christ, the Righteous One!

NOTES AND REFLECTIONS

NOTES AND REFLECTIONS

NOTES AND REFLECTIONS

CHAPTER 6

JESUS – THE PRINCE OF PEACE

Peace. In a world filled with chaos and confusion, where do we go to find it? More than that, whom do we go to receive it? We all have a need for peace in our lives – peace with God, peace with others and peace with ourselves. There are many distractions in our world that hinder us from entering into peace. I'm not just talking about being in a peaceful, dreamy state; the peace that I am speaking of is that of a heart at rest, despite whatever circumstances are coming against the human heart. Apart from Christ, there is no peace.

For most of my life, there was a distinct absence of peace. I enjoyed excitement and would create very chaotic situations. I always thought that to be peaceful would be boring, and I hated to be bored. As a result of this mindset, relationships in my life suffered the damage that my recklessness caused. Even though I was a Christian, I did not fully understand the precious fact that I had peace with God through Jesus Christ my Lord. I seldom lived at peace with others because I was not at peace with myself. I suffered from a guilty conscious because of all the sin in my life and the sad truth is that many hurting people go on to hurt others. I didn't want to intentionally hurt those that I loved, but my actions would cause harm to others. A raging storm was always brewing in my heart, and even if I succeeded at getting what I wanted, I could not find lasting joy in whatever it was I had acquired. That all changed when Jesus whispered peace into my soul. My heart has been transformed!

Isaiah 9:6 says, *For to us a child is born, to us a son is given, and the government will be on his shoulders. And he will be called Wonderful Counselor, Mighty God, Everlasting Father,* **Prince of Peace.** Jesus brings us peace when the world brings us alarm. Just the mention of Christ's name delivers to me a peace that words cannot describe and that no one can take away. Christ in me is my peace. In John 14:27, Jesus said the following: *Peace I leave with you; my peace I give you. I do not give to you as the world gives. Do not let your hearts be troubled and do not be afraid.* Apart from Christ, there is much to fear. But in Christ, there is no reason to fear. Realizing that God is ultimately in control is comforting. Knowing the God who is in control is spectacular!

Let me share an account in the gospel of Mark when Jesus brought stillness into a raging storm. It is found in Mark 4:35-41: *That day when evening came, he said to his disciples, "Let us go over to the other side." Leaving the crowd behind, they took him along, just as he was, in the boat. There were also other boats with him. A furious squall came up, and the waves broke over the boat, so that it was nearly swamped. Jesus was in the stern, sleeping on a cushion. The disciples woke him and said to him, "Teacher, don't you care if we drown?" He got up, rebuked the wind and said to the waves, "Quiet! Be still!" Then the wind died down and it was completely calm. He said to his disciples, "Why are you so afraid? Do you still have no faith?" They were terrified and asked each other, "Who is this? Even the wind and the waves obey him!"* That is what Christ Jesus has done with my heart. He has stilled the "furious squall" that was damaging my life and the lives of those around me. When the waves were dragging me under the sea of depression and fear, Jesus made the waters calm. I am not saying that I never encounter storms in my life; the truth is that I do. But during those storms my heart is at rest because the Prince of Peace is present with me in the midst of them.

For years I tried to quiet the storm by using marijuana. What a deception this was! Sure, I would find temporary relief – like one putting a band aid on a gaping wound! Coping with the storms of life with a bottle of wine or an illegal substance is not true peace. This is sleepwalking your way through life, as one goes around groping in the darkness. Psalm 34:8 says, *Taste and see that the Lord is good; blessed is the man who takes refuge in him.* I have tried what the world offers, and I have tasted of the peace that Jesus gives. Christ's offer is more supreme and is truly satisfying.

Jesus is the Prince of Peace. When He is living on the inside of you, you have all you need. Nothing else can add to what He gives us generously. We can choose to reject His offer of salvation and forfeit our chance for security, or we can simply choose to receive His love and mercy. Psalm 34:5-10 says, *Your love, O Lord, reaches to the heavens, your faithfulness to the skies. Your righteousness is like the mighty mountains, your justice like the great deep. O Lord, you preserve both man and beast. How priceless is your unfailing love! Both high and low among men find refuge in the shadow of your wings. They feast on the abundance of your house; you give them drink from your river of delights. For with you is the fountain of life; in your light we see light. Continue your love to those who know you, your righteousness to the upright in heart.* If you have not yet received the Prince of Peace into your heart and life, then I urge you to ask Him to come in. Peace is just one word away – Jesus!

NOTES AND REFLECTIONS

NOTES AND REFLECTIONS

NOTES AND REFLECTIONS

CHAPTER 7

JESUS – EL SHADDAI

One of the many names for God is El Shaddai, which means "the God who is sufficient." Another way of interpreting this beautiful name is "the God who is more than enough." This is one of the Hebrew names for God and holds great promise for those of us who struggle in this life. It is also a great eye-opener for those who believe they are "self-sufficient" and do not need God in their lives. The name El Shaddai is translated "God Almighty." In Genesis 17:1 we read, *When Abram was ninety-nine years old, the Lord God appeared to him and said, "I am God Almighty; walk before me and be blameless."*

In this verse, the Hebrew meaning for God Almighty is El Shaddai, the God who is sufficient. Because Jesus is one with God the Father (see John 10:30), He can rightfully use this name as one of His own. Therefore, for this chapter, we are going to look at how Jesus is all-sufficient and all that we need in this life.

For most of my life, I tried to do things my own way, without giving careful attention to what God would have me do. Now, praise God, I know that it is Jesus who is my Lord and, as such, is the One who has every right to direct my steps and author my life. Jesus' plan for my life and yours is good; but, we can go against His plan and live as though we are independent of Him. This is a tragic choice because Christ says in John 15:5b, *apart from me you can do nothing.* In this context, Jesus is speaking of "bearing fruit" unto God – a life with meaning and purpose in Him. As a Believer, I am learning that when I do things in my own strength and try to do good things apart from Jesus, those things do not produce the quality of excellence that I desire. Jesus is a God of excellence. Would it not be wiser to allow Him to live through me and do the work? I am simply the instrument that He chooses to work through – all of my success is what He has done. How can I take credit for His work? This attitude requires humility, the kind of humility that Jesus has.

My pastor calls this "dependency on Christ," and he is absolutely correct. Knowing that Jesus is all-sufficient and does not need my futile efforts, releases me from the pressure to "perform" well as a Christian. Thus, it is the all-sufficient One who brings about excellent things in and through me. To have the idea that we need to be successful in order to have a happy life is an error of judgment. Jesus is the Head of the Church, and many forget to acknowledge that it is He who builds us up and gets us to where we ought to be. He is the One in control and even if we think we could do a better job of things, the truth is that we cannot. Jesus sees the "big picture" and knows things that we simply do not know or understand at this time. Allowing Him to lead me requires faith and trust. Similarly, we have to allow Him to do His work and not resist what His Spirit is trying to do in us. We can offer resistance, but in such a case we are only hurting ourselves and others. He has your best interest at heart, as well as the best interest of the Church. This is about Him building His Kingdom, for He said in Matthew 16:18 that it is He who builds His Church. He is sufficient enough to do the job for us, and we can enjoy watching Him as He works so beautifully in us to make something of excellence and something that will last for all eternity.

If you ever had a loved one taken from you, or you have been separated from those you care about, Christ is enough! Your life does not have to fall to pieces because of tragic circumstances. When a person has Jesus as their Savior, His precious Spirit lives on the inside of them. And what a beautiful Spirit He is! The Holy Spirit is loving, gentle, tender and comforting. I know the gut-wrenching pain of losing a spouse in death and having my children taken from me. Apart from Christ, the grief would have been so drastic that it would have taken my very life. The only One who can give us true comfort in such times is God – the Father, the Son, and the Holy Spirit – one God who is capable of doing what no human being can do. Nothing is impossible with Jehovah God – **absolutely nothing**! In Christ, we have all we could ever need to soar in this life. A good career, a successful job title, a bank account with enormous numbers in it, designer clothes, nice cars, beautiful houses, and whatever else one may accumulate does not equate success. Can you take these things with you when you die? Will they offer you a lasting comfort in times of trial and distress? Can they redeem your soul from hell and the grave? Most assuredly, they cannot! Jesus Christ, El Shaddai, can. He is the only One who can, and when this life is over, the only thing that will matter is if we have received Him into our hearts as Savior and Lord. This life will end – no one lives forever. What happens next? These are not easy questions to ask, but they are necessary. Satan is blinding the world to the truth about eternity. Jesus, through the awesome power of His Holy Spirit, is at work in the world to reach people and to point them to the Savior. But just look at all the distractions the enemy of our souls has given to the world! I pray that even now, as you read this chapter, the Spirit of the living God would touch your heart and open your eyes to see your need for Jesus, El Shaddai.

Allow me to share a story with you that demonstrates how Jesus is El Shaddai in our personal lives. My aunt (her name is Debbie) lived with her mother (my grandmother) for most of her life. When my grandfather passed away, Debbie and her mom moved in together and took care of each other. They shared their income with each other, as well as supported each other in everyday life. Debbie had made the choice years prior that she would not marry, because her desire was to take care of my grandmother. Nanny was quite sick with a bad heart, and around the time of her death, they were in financial debt. The Lord gave an unexpected financial blessing to them through my other aunt, my grandmother's sister. Debbie said, "Look, Lord! Now we can pay off our debt. Thank you." The Lord then spoke back to my aunt and said, "Your mother is going to die." "Oh no," Debbie replied. She tried to shake it off and paid off the debt that they had.

Not too long after that, my grandmother died in hospital and Debbie felt that she would be left all alone. In her grief, she was not handling her affairs very well. She had to move out of the lovely apartment that they shared, but she was too grief-stricken to make arrangements for that. Jesus used my mother greatly to find her a place to live that was close to our family. God often uses other people to minister to us, but we often look at that person for stability instead of God. Jesus took care of my aunt the same way that a husband would care and provide for a wife. The Lord was intricately involved in Debbie's circumstances and demonstrated that He is El Shaddai, the God who is sufficient. Debbie now has a lovely home and a beautiful relationship with Christ. The Lord knows those that are His, and He cares for them.

The Lord wants to be the same God for you that He is for Debbie. He wants to care for you and be the One you call upon for help in times of loneliness, fear, anxiety, depression, grief and despair. He will come into your life and His grace will minister to your particular set of circumstances. I pray that you will know El Shaddai personally; He will not disappoint you!

NOTES AND REFLECTIONS

NOTES AND REFLECTIONS

NOTES AND REFLECTIONS

CHAPTER 8

JESUS – A REFUGE FOR CHILDREN

Oh, the love that Jesus has for the little ones! I have the privilege of teaching Sunday School at my church, and I love to see the responses of the children when they are told how much Jesus loves them.

I asked four children the following question: Who is Jesus to you? Here were their responses:

Will says (age 5) "Jesus loves me, he died on the cross, he rose again. I like that he made the world, flowers our home. He helped me long ago when I needed to talk to my friends about hitting me and running into me."

Nerida (age 9) says: "he is someone I can rely on and he is my friend. He helps me when I need it and he is someone who always loves me."

Hannah (age 13) "A friend, someone I have relied on since the moment I was born and until the moment my life ends. He's always there for me. To comfort me, to make me smile and to help me, just like my friends at school."

Lydia (age 8) "My dad, I love him. He will listen to my every prayer. He helps me make the right decision. I always ask him what to do, (only if it's necessary) and most of the time everything turns out great! God is my friend; not only my friend, my dad as well."

What precious responses! In Matthew 19:13-15, we read this: *Then little children were brought to Jesus for him to place His hands on them and pray for them. But the disciples rebuked those who brought them. Jesus said, "Let the little children come to me, and do not hinder them, for the kingdom of heaven belongs to such as these." When he had placed his hands on them, he went on from there.*

When I was four years old, I gave my heart to Jesus. How I loved Him, and I knew that He loved me. He blessed me with a wonderful family, and I was raised with knowledge of God. Jesus was my best friend. As I became a teenager, I started to drift away from Him and became very rebellious. This continued on into my twenties until I realized how much I missed sharing my life with the Lord. He forgave all my sin and has restored my mind. I love Him even more now than I did as a child. But I can remember being a child and feeling absolutely safe because I knew that Jesus was in control. Having child-like faith, even as an adult, is very precious to God.

In Matthew 18:1-4 we read the following: *At that time the disciples came to Jesus and asked, "Who is greatest in the kingdom of heaven?" He called a little child and had him stand among them. And he said, "I tell you the truth, unless you change and become like little children, you will never enter the kingdom of heaven. Therefore, whoever humbles himself like this child is greatest in the kingdom of heaven."* This is what I meant when I wrote about child-like faith. Children believe from their heart without demanding to see evidence – this is true faith. Jesus said that we need that same kind of faith if we are going to see the Kingdom of Heaven. Faith is taking God at His Word, despite what the circumstances may look like.

There are some people who, sadly, have endured a miserable childhood. Abuse and neglect may have been what you have experienced at one time or another. Jesus cares! He cared then, and He cares now. Undoubtedly, some will ask, "If God really loved me, why do I have to go through all of this? Why did He allow me to live through such a miserable childhood?" I used to have a habit of blaming God when I encountered painful circumstances. But, now that I continue to study His Word, I realize that sin is responsible, not God. This is a fallen world at the present time, and God has given us a free-will. If you have been hurt in your childhood, then I encourage you to seek Christ Jesus for healing. He is able to heal you in the deepest regions of your soul. Rather than blame God, embrace Him and His plan for your life. His plan for your life is good, not harmful. (see Jeremiah 29:11) When you encounter a storm in your life, please know that if you have received Jesus as your Savior, He is right there with you in that storm.

So I challenge you – become like a child today and receive the good news of salvation! Jesus is waiting for you, and He loves you.

NOTES AND REFLECTIONS

NOTES AND REFLECTIONS

NOTES AND REFLECTIONS

CHAPTER 9

JESUS – THE WORD OF GOD

One of the names of Jesus is the "Word." We see this in John 1:1-2: *In the beginning was the Word, and the Word was with God, and the Word was God. He was with God in the beginning.* Jesus is the living Word of God. I would like to examine the Word of God, or the Bible, in detail.

I have met people who believe that the Bible is just a bunch of historical writings, not the living, inspired Word of God. This is simply untrue. 2 Peter 1:21 says, *For prophecy never had its origin in the will of man, but men spoke from God as they were carried along by the Holy Spirit.* And again, 2 Timothy 3:16-17 declares, *All Scripture is God-breathed and is useful for teaching, rebuking, correcting and training in righteousness, so that the man of God may be thoroughly equipped for every good work.* We see from this verse that the Word of God is useful for the believer to be "thoroughly equipped for every good work." What a precious gift that God has given us – His Holy Word!

The Lord has used His Word mightily in my life throughout the years. It is the standard of truth for our lives and, because of it, I am able to distinguish God's reality from the lies of the world and Satan. There has to be a standard by which we live. God's Word burns so deeply within my heart that any teaching that I hear that is not in step with the truth of God's Word, is dismissed in my mind. Since I became a student of the Word of God, my thoughts are more clear and organized. Christ Jesus, as previously mentioned, is the Word of God, and it is the Lord who has healed my mind and set me free. It is a tragic shame when many who profess Christianity do not give full attention to the Word of God. God says in Hosea 4:6 the following: *my people are destroyed from lack of knowledge.* God in His infinite love and mercy has given us the answers to all of life's meaningful questions in the Bible, a book that has been preserved for thousands of years. God ensured that these ancient writings, which apply to our lives no matter how many centuries have passed (for God's Word does not change from generation to generation – the world may change, but His Word remains true and is applicable for today), building us up and teaching us about Himself. The world needs a standard of truth.

My prayer for my nation is that we would return to the God who formed us and brought us together into this beautiful land. Compromising our Biblical values for the sake of pleasing those who choose to live a life apart from God is a dangerous thing. The question is, how long will God allow this to continue? How long will we continue to ignore His warning and His leading? It is my prayer for the Church that we would rise up and hold fast to the Word of Life, which has the answers to all the problems our world is facing.

There is also the aspect of the Christian's personal walk with God. The more we read God's Word and understand His holiness and delight in His ways, the more our soul prospers. The Apostle John writes in 3 John 1:2, *Dear friend, I pray that you may enjoy good health and that all may go well with you, even as your soul is getting along well.* Having a personal relationship with Jesus Christ is paramount for a healthy soul. True prosperity is enjoying the goodness of God in the land of the living. Anything anyone would ever need is found in the Scriptures. If reading the Bible is something new to you, you are not alone. Every student of God's Word had to begin somewhere. There are commentaries and resources available to you to assist in your study. In light of the fact that Jesus is the Word of God, whenever you read His Word, you are spending time with the Lord. If you are a new believer in Christ, then I recommend that you begin in the New Testament. The Old Testament is just as important, but for the new Christian it is important for you to have an understanding of the New Covenant of Grace and to learn about the life of Christ.

Hebrews 4:12 is a fascinating perspective on God's Holy Word. It reads, *For the word of God is living and active. Sharper than any double-edged sword, it penetrates even to dividing soul and spirit, joints and marrow; it judges the thoughts and attitudes of the heart.* The word of God is like a mirror for us. When we examine ourselves in light of God's Word, we understand if something in our lives is out of balance with Him. This is how we learn and grow in obedience to Christ. The problem is that our flesh likes what is comfortable and easy. It does not like to be challenged. Our spirit, on the other hand, longs for God's holiness and desires to be like Him. The Word of God, when applied to our lives, brings about radical changes in our thoughts and behaviors.

Those of us who have accepted Jesus as our Lord should pray fervently that He would grant us a deep love and longing for His Word. How I have come to love and respect His Word more than life itself! It is nourishment for the deepest regions of my soul. I know and am convinced that God's Word can penetrate the hardest of hearts and bring healing to the broken-hearted. Jesus sees who you really are – nothing is hidden from His sight. For the most part, people see of us what we want them to see. Jesus sees it all, and He cares. When I first became intimately acquainted with Jesus, I would be embarrassed at times concerning my own vulnerability. But He wouldn't leave me – He wouldn't give up on me. His strength and ability to perform miraculous things on my behalf has been proven time and time again. He's trustworthy, and my heart is at rest in His presence – not because I am such a lovely person, but because He is lovely in me! He is so radiant and victorious that I cannot possibly do Him justice with words. My prayer is that you would know Jesus yourself. Revelation 19:13 says, *He is dressed in a robe dipped in blood, and his name is the Word of God.* This is speaking of the time when Christ returns to the earth to set up His millennial kingdom. His name has not changed – Jesus is the Word of God!

NOTES AND REFLECTIONS

NOTES AND REFLECTIONS

NOTES AND REFLECTIONS

CHAPTER 10

JESUS – DIVINE LOVE

1 John 4:8 Whoever does not love does not know God, **because God is love.**

Jesus is the exact representation of love. His very nature and character encompasses all that love is supposed to be – and He offers His love to all of us. The gospels repeatedly demonstrate the way that Jesus loved people while He was on the earth, and that same love still resonates today and forever. Love such as this is too powerful for our finite minds to comprehend, yet it is the comfort for believers in Christ.

Let us look at the Biblical definition of love. It is found in 1 Corinthians 13:4-8b: *Love is patient, love is kind. It does not envy, it does not boast, it is not proud. It is not rude, it is not self-seeking, it is not easily angered, it keeps no record of wrongs. Love does not delight in evil but rejoices with the truth. It always protects, always trusts, always hopes, always perseveres. Love never fails.* This is the hallmark of Christ's love for us. Jesus does not just love those who love Him; He loves the whole world and calls to the unsaved heart and whispers His love to them. Because the Lord is a gentleman, He will not force Himself on anyone who is unwilling to receive His love, but He loves them just the same. It has been the love of Christ that has brought me through many a dark hour.

Since I was a young teenager, I deeply wanted the love of others, especially that of the opposite sex. I didn't have the insight into God's unconditional love for me, so I was hungry for love from other boys. As I grew older, I would do some pretty outrageous things to try and gain love from other men. I was often left feeling unfulfilled because of the way I would pursue attention from men. When my late husband and I first began seeing each other, I would lie and manipulate to get him to love me, the way I felt that I deserved to be loved. Had I had revelation in my heart of the way Jesus loved and accepted me, things would have been a whole lot different. But I seldom ever read the Bible to know God's truth for myself, nor had I "experienced" Christ's love at that point. Jesus has set me free from that cycle of torment, and now I am completely in love with Jesus, and I am content to know that He loves me back. The love that He and I share is pure and beautiful, and He is willing to share that love with all who call upon His name for salvation. It is a beautiful thing to know that you are loved by someone so great, for indeed there is no one greater than God. David says in Psalm 8:4, *what is man that you are mindful of him, the son of man that you should care for him?* Even during those times when I am completely "unlovable," Jesus loves me. He loves me when my behavior is good, and He loves me when my behavior is less than perfect. His love for me never changes.

If you are wondering if there is anything you can do to cause Christ to love you less, let me assure you that there isn't. I have sunk into the depths of sin many times when I was younger, before I became a serious student of the Word of God; before I gave my life to Him completely. I am a former drug addict, and the behaviors that go along with that are very damaging. I lied, stole, exchanged sex for drugs and many other things that I will not even mention. But when the reality of Christ's love became revelation into my spirit, that all changed. I determined to respond to His love by a complete dedication of my life to His service. His love has set me free in more ways than I can mention, and I am forever in His heart. He is willing and able to do the same for you. If you are worn out and tired of the burdens you are carrying, give them to the Lord. In Matthew 11:28-30, Jesus says the following: *Come to me, all you who are weary and burdened, and I will give you rest. Take my yoke upon you and learn from me, for I am gentle and humble in heart, and you will find rest for your souls. For my yoke is easy and my burden is light.*

If you have not yet received Jesus as your Lord and Savior, then listen carefully – He is calling your name! He is inviting you into His presence and offering you eternal life. His love will not disappoint you. He has already demonstrated His love for you at the cross. Jesus said in John 15:13,

Greater love has no one than this, that he lay down his life for his friends. Jesus laid down His life for you, taking all of the sins of the world upon Himself, dying on the cross to pay our debt. He took the punishment that we deserved, and it was His love that held Him to the cross – not the nails! Jesus knows all your fears, worries, weaknesses and heartaches, and He cares about every detail of your life. You can know love in all its fullness by simply receiving the Lord into your heart. I plead with you not to put this off, for none of us are guaranteed our next breath of life. To reject Christ is to spend eternity separated from God. However, when we receive Jesus into our hearts and lives, eternal life is ours. John 3:16 says, *For God so loved the world that he gave his one and only Son, that whoever believes in him shall not perish but have eternal life.* You have nothing to lose and everything to gain! Receive Christ's love today!

NOTES AND REFLECTIONS

NOTES AND REFLECTIONS

NOTES AND REFLECTIONS

CHAPTER 11

JESUS – THE GREAT HIGH PRIEST

If you own a Bible, you will notice that there are two sections – The Old Testament and The New Testament. Another way you may identify with these two sections are the Old Covenant and the New Covenant. I will briefly explain both to you.

In the Old Covenant, animal sacrifices were required to cover over the sins of the Jewish people. The high priest would offer these sacrifices once a year for the unintentional sins of the people. The exact requirements are recorded in the book of the law in the Old Testament. The high priest who served at the alter would have to offer a sacrifice for his own sins, then again for the sins of the people. This was a shadow of what Christ would ultimately do to bring about a new covenant – one that was sealed in His own blood. Because of Christ's death on the cross as the final sacrifice once and for all, animal sacrifice is no longer required. He is the Lamb without spot or defect, a perfect sacrifice that pleased God. For all who receive His sacrifice by inviting Jesus into their hearts, they are saved with a salvation that can never be taken away.

Jesus is the mediator of our new covenant, and He is a High Priest forever. Hebrews 8:6 tells us: *But the ministry Jesus has received is as superior to theirs as the covenant of which he is mediator is superior to the old one, and it is founded on better promises.* Hebrews chapter 8 details how Jesus, the High Priest of a new covenant, has fulfilled the will of God concerning our salvation. Let me share Hebrews 8:8-13 with you: *But God found fault with the people and said: "The time is coming, declares the Lord, when I will make a new covenant with the house of Israel and with the house of Judah. It will not be like the covenant I made with their forefathers when I took them by the hand to lead them out of Egypt, because they did not remain faithful to my covenant, and I turned away from them, declares the Lord. This is the covenant I will make with the house of Israel after that time, declares the Lord. I will put my laws in their minds and write them on their hearts. I will be their God, and they will be my people. No longer will a man teach his neighbor, or a man his brother, saying, 'Know the Lord,' because they will all know me, from the least of them to the greatest. For I will forgive their wickedness and remember their sins no more." By calling this covenant "new," he has made the first one obsolete; and what is obsolete and aging will soon disappear.*

Jesus is now seated at the right hand of God the Father, and He is the High Priest of the new covenant based on grace. Grace is the underserved or unmerited favor of God. Hebrews 10:11-14 compares the old covenant of animal sacrifices to the new covenant that God has given through His Son, Jesus: *Day after day every priest stands and performs his religious duties; again and again he offers the same sacrifices, which can never take away sins. But when this priest* (Jesus) *had offered for all time one sacrifice for sins, he sat down at the right hand of God. Since that time he waits for his enemies to be made his footstool,* **because by one sacrifice he has made perfect forever those who are being made holy**.

None of us could honestly say that we have followed the Ten Commandments perfectly. Every one has fallen short of the glory of God (Romans 3:23). The Ten Commandments were to show mankind that we could never fully obey God and live up to His standard of perfection. It was meant to point us to the Savior, who indeed fulfilled the law and was able to be the perfect sacrifice, once and for all, for sins. The new covenant is available to everyone, both Jews and Gentiles alike. Colossians 1:27 says, *To them God has chosen to make known among the Gentiles the glorious riches of this mystery, which is Christ in you, the hope of glory.* When we receive Jesus as our personal Lord and Savior, then His Spirit comes to live on the inside of us. When we allow Christ in us to live through us, we find that we do those things that please God. We are still not perfect, because all of us stumble at times; however, we are no longer under the sentence of death – death meaning eternal separation from God in the Lake of Fire.

When speaking of temptation to sin, there is a comforting passage that I would love to share with you. Hebrews 4:14-16 tells us the following: *Therefore, since we have a great high priest who has gone through the heavens, Jesus the Son of God, let us hold firmly to the faith we profess.* **For we do not have a high priest who is unable to sympathize with our weaknesses, but we have one who has been tempted in every way, just as we are – yet was without sin.** *Let us then approach the throne of grace with confidence, so that we may receive mercy and find grace to help us in our time of need.*

My life has not always been the way it is now. Many times I have fallen into the deep, dark pit of sin and misery; yet, Jesus, the Great High Priest, rescued me and helped me. During those times when I would indulge in sin, I would have difficulty approaching the Throne of God in prayer with confidence because I was so ashamed of my conduct. But that is precisely what we are supposed to do – approach the Throne of Grace and receive mercy and help. Shutting Jesus out of our lives is the worst tragedy imaginable, because we can only get real help from Jesus. Romans 8:1-2 tells us, *Therefore, there is now no condemnation for those who are in Christ Jesus, because the law of the Spirit of life set me free from the law of sin and death.*

If you have received Jesus as your Savior, then you are covered in His blood – and you are clean. God the Father, when He looks at me, does not see Melody the "sinner." He sees someone who has been purchased by Christ with his own blood and, whether or not I feel like it, I am now a saint. That is my position as a daughter of the Most High God, and that will never change no matter how I perform as a Christian. Having said that, when our hearts are filled with the love of God, we cannot help but live and do better than we did before we were Born Again. God is at work conforming us into the image of His Son, Jesus Christ. One day, either when we die or when Jesus comes back for us, we will be perfect, as He is. This is a day I look forward to with all my heart. In the meantime, I am satisfied to know that Jesus is the Great High Priest!

NOTES AND REFLECTIONS

NOTES AND REFLECTIONS

NOTES AND REFLECTIONS

CHAPTER 12

JESUS – THE TENDER SHEPHERD

Jesus, in the Gospel of John, identifies Himself as the good shepherd. (John 10:11) How does this apply to the Believer's life today? Those of us who put our faith and trust in Christ for salvation are the sheep. We belong to Jesus, the good shepherd. Sheep have a tendency to wander off – but Jesus searches for them to bring them back into the fold. No one who believes in Jesus is lost; those who have rejected Him are lost. I pray that you will decide to believe in Jesus for salvation and become one of His sheep. When speaking of sheep and how they tend to wander off, let's consider what Jesus said in Matthew 18:12-14: *What do you think? If a man owns a hundred sheep, and one of them wanders away, will he not leave the ninety-nine on the hills and go to look for the one that wandered off? And if he finds it, I tell you the truth, he is happier about that one sheep than about the ninety-nine that did not wander off. In the same way your Father in heaven is not willing that any of these little ones should be lost.*

The beginning of the 23rd Psalm is: *The Lord is my shepherd, I shall not be in want.* Then in verse 4 the psalmist writes, *Even though I walk through the valley of the shadow of death, I will fear no evil, for you are with me;* **your rod and your staff, they comfort me**. Many do not understand the significance of the rod and the staff. Shepherds always had two articles with them to assist them in their job – a rod and a staff. Many people, including Christians, believe that the rod is used to "beat" the sheep back in line. This is not true. The rod was actually for protection – to beat off the wolves who would attempt to harm the sheep! And the staff was used to gently guide the sheep back into the fold where they belong. This is why the psalmist said that the Lord's rod and staff were a comfort to him.

Let's take a look at how Jesus identified Himself in John chapter 10. In Verses 11-18, Jesus said the following: *I am the good shepherd. The good shepherd lays down his life for the sheep. The hired hand is not the shepherd who owns the sheep. So when he sees the wolf coming, he abandons the sheep and runs away. Then the wolf attacks the flock and scatters it. The man runs away because he is a hired hand and cares nothing for the sheep. I am the good shepherd; I know my sheep and my sheep know me – just as the Father knows me and I know the Father – and I lay down my life for the sheep. I have other sheep that are not of this sheep pen. I must bring them also. They too will listen to my voice, and there shall be one flock and one shepherd. The reason my Father loves me is that I lay down my life – only to take it up again. No one takes it from me, but I lay it down of my own accord. I have authority to lay it down and authority to take it up again. This command I received from my Father.* Jesus, the Good Shepherd, has graciously laid down His life for His sheep at Calvary. He died on the cross, taking our sins upon Himself, and is offering everyone everywhere forgiveness through His Name. All we have to do is believe and receive. We believe on Jesus, and then we receive salvation. This is what John 3:16 promises. He arose from the grave three days later and is now alive forever more.

If you are reading this book and you have not yet received Christ Jesus as your Lord and Savior, then you are searching. You are searching for something or someone to believe in that will make sense. Jesus is that Someone, and He is waiting for you. He wants to be your Shepherd and lead you along the paths of righteousness for his Name's sake. (see Psalm 23) He has been ever so faithful in His love for me, even though I have not always been faithful in my love for Him. Many times I have done some very selfish and sinful things, but He has never abandoned me. This is because I am one of His sheep. More than that, when I've been flat out lost, He has found me. His Word has proven to be true over and over in my life.

There was a time when I was involved in a very unhealthy relationship. I was in sin and very miserable. I knew what God wanted in my life, and this man had no role to play in the plans that Jesus had for me and my life. This relationship was very toxic to me and was poisoning my spirit. I wanted freedom, but I chose to remain in this situation. I would cry out to

Jesus over and over for deliverance until my pastor pointed out something to me that was very true. He shared with me that Jesus had already set me free from this situation when He died for me, and I am no longer a slave of sin. This was significant information for me to grasp. At first, I did not feel very free. But now the truth of what he said stirs in my heart and is a truth well-established in my spirit. Jesus, the tender and loving Shepherd, removed me from that situation by giving me the strength to end the relationship. God doesn't just tell us to do something and then leave us powerless to do it. Jesus living in me and through me keeps me strong – it's His strength, not my own, that gets me through each and every day. I pray you will have the same strength made available to you in Jesus Christ.

By God's grace, I am at a point in my life where Jesus is more than enough. I am content to remain devoted to Him in body and spirit, and I am passionate about Him for I know that He is passionate about me. I love Him with all my heart, soul, mind and strength. This is why I am writing this book. I want everyone to experience the love that Jesus has for them. He loves you whether you are rich or poor. He loves you even if you do not love yourself. He is there for all those who are broken, lost and hurting. Family may abandon you; friends may abuse you; society may frown upon you – but Jesus cares deeply for your life. He will never leave us nor forsake us. (Hebrews 13:5) Listen. Do you hear Him calling your name? Do you see Him as He delights in you? He wants you to be His very own. He wants to be the Shepherd of your soul. We've already established in chapter 1 that He created you. Who better knows you than the One who created you for Himself? You have a place in His heart, and the invitation is wide open for you to enter into His rest. You were created with a purpose that far exceeds anything you could ever have expected. To be part of God's kingdom is to be part of something great – there is nothing greater than belonging to God. There is nothing as important as having your destiny fulfilled in His precious plan. Open wide your heart for the King to enter in!

Not only does Jesus refer to Himself as the Good Shepherd, but He also calls Himself the "gate" for the sheep in John chapter 10. Verses 7-10 says, *Therefore Jesus said again, "I tell you the truth. I am the gate for the sheep. All who ever came before me were thieves and robbers, but the sheep did not listen to them. I am the gate; whoever enters through me will be saved. He will come in and go out, and find pasture. The thief comes only to steal and kill and destroy; I have come that they may have life, and have it to the full.* The thief is the devil, and Jesus is very correct when He tells us that he comes to steal and kill and destroy. There is nothing life-giving about Satan – he loves only what causes harm to mankind. Jesus, on the other hand, came to give us life to the full.

The heart of Jesus is so tender and loving. He is kind, caring and compassionate. For those of us who have trusted in Him for salvation, we are His treasured possession. And He desires for everyone to have eternal life through Him. There is no other way. Jesus alone is the Way, the Truth and the Life (see John 14:6) God has made a way for us to escape eternal separation from His presence and that way is through His Son, Jesus. Knowing that Jesus watches over me and guards me with His rod and guides me with His staff allows me to sleep well at night. He is my tender Shepherd!

NOTES AND REFLECTIONS

NOTES AND REFLECTIONS

NOTES AND REFLECTIONS

CHAPTER 13

JESUS – IMMANUEL

Matthew 1:23 "The virgin will be with child and will give birth to a son, and they will call him Immanuel" – which means, "God with us."

Jesus remains faithful to His Name Immanuel, for He was both with us when He was alive on the earth, and He remains in the hearts of those who have put their faith in Him. He is "God with us."

One of the fears that use to hold me fast was the fear of being alone. The reality that Christ was with me on all occasions seemed to allude me. Perhaps this is because I couldn't see Him. However, 2 Corinthians 5:7 tell us, *We live by faith, not by sight.* The reality of God's presence is so real to me now that I never feel alone – at least not to the extent that I use to. Whenever I start to feel alone, I remind myself of God's Word that Jesus is Immanuel, God with us. Because His Spirit lives on the inside of me, I am never alone! I pray that those of you who often feel alone and rejected will be blessed by this chapter.

The disciples enjoyed three years of following Jesus as He was involved in His earthly ministry. However, shortly before His arrest and crucifixion, He told them plainly that He would be going away. Jesus says in John 14:16-18 the following: *And I will ask the Father, and he will give you another Counselor to be with you forever – the Spirit of truth. The world cannot accept him, because it neither sees him nor knows him. But you know him, for he lives with you and will be in you. I will not leave you as orphans; I will come to you.* The Holy Spirit is the Spirit of our Lord Jesus and this is how we know that Christ is still Immanuel, for He lives on the inside of us who believe.

On June 28, 2008, my husband died of a massive heart attack on his way to work. I was 28 years old at the time. My initial response was that of sorrow and fear – the fear of being alone. As I began preparations for his funeral, I realized that there was a strength inside me that was not my own. I knew then that it was the Lord who was carrying me through the agony of the loss of a loved one. I knew then what Immanuel, God with us, actually meant. Without Jesus I am nothing. But because of Jesus, I can do all things through Him who strengthens me. (Philippians 4:13) I cannot possibly begin to describe to you all that Jesus has done in me and for me. He has changed my very heart from one that used to be stubborn and cold to one that is tender and loving. Romans 8:29-30 says, *For those God foreknew he also predestined to be conformed to the likeness of his Son, that he might be the firstborn among many brothers. And those he predestined, he also called; those he called, he also justified; those he justified, he also glorified.* Believers in Christ Jesus are being changed from glory to glory to be conformed into the likeness of Jesus.

Let's look at some reasons why some would reject the gracious offer that Jesus gives us, the offer of His abiding presence in their lives. One reason I can think of is accountability. By receiving Jesus as Lord of our lives, there must be submission to His Lordship. Many people want to be "independent" and believe that they only need themselves to be successful. Submitting to Jesus means growing in dependence on Him, not on our own strength and abilities. Please don't misunderstand me – God gives us gifts to use for His glory. But self-sufficiency is dangerous, despite what the world may teach regarding that. God is all-sufficient, and we must come to a place where His will is the supreme deciding factor for our attitudes, thoughts and behaviors. This requires humility.

Another reason some reject Christ is disbelief. With all the false teachers and religions that are in the world today, is it any wonder that people are confused about which way is the right way? Satan has busied himself with deceiving people into believing that they do not need the Cross of Calvary. Many people think, "I'm a good person. That's all that matters." If our good works could save us, then why did Jesus die? We are not justified in God's sight by good works, but by grace through faith in the Son of God.

Ephesians 2:8-9 explains it this way: *For it is by grace you have been saved, through faith – **and this not from yourselves, it is the gift of God – not by works, so that no one can boast**.* We see from this passage that it is Jesus who has met the requirements of perfection, thereby being our only hope of salvation. His sacrifice is perfect and complete, and it is the blood of Jesus applied to our lives that save us. Only then will we experience Immanuel in all His fullness!

NOTES AND REFLECTIONS

NOTES AND REFLECTIONS

NOTES AND REFLECTIONS

CHAPTER 14

JESUS – THE SOON COMING KING

By now we have covered a lot concerning Jesus. We have looked at who He is in detail, and we have examined what the Scriptures say concerning His life. I have shared with you how He is at the right hand of God and is alive forever more. But what happens next? Will Jesus ever return to earth and reign? The answer is yes! A day, in the not too distant future, Jesus will return to earth to establish His Kingdom and reign forever. When the angel came to Mary to announce that she would give birth to a Son, he foretold what His future destiny would be. Luke 1:30-33 says, *But the angel said to her, "Do not be afraid, Mary, you have found favor with God. You will be with child and give birth to a son, and you are to give him the name Jesus. He will be great and will be called the Son of the Most High. **The Lord God will give him the throne of his father David, and he will reign over the house of Jacob forever; his kingdom will never end."***

Gabriel's promise was not fulfilled during Jesus first coming, for He had to die and be raised to life again for the salvation of mankind. He ascended into heaven and is now at the Father's right hand. God is waiting for people to receive Jesus into their hearts, and He is being very kind and patient with the lost because His desire is that everyone should be saved. 2 Peter 3:9 tells us, *The Lord is not slow in keeping his promise, as some understand slowness. He is patient with you, not wanting anyone to perish, but everyone to come to repentance.* However, the day will come when He will tarry no more, and then Gabriel's words to Mary will be fulfilled. What a different world this will be when Jesus is here and reigning over it! You may read of the future of Christ's return and what the outcome will be for mankind in Revelation chapters 19-22. I would strongly encourage you to read it prayerfully.

Before Christ returns to earth at the Second Coming, there is one very important event that will take place first. This event is known as the Rapture. This is when Jesus descends from heaven in the clouds to gather together in the sky all those who have placed their faith in Him for salvation. This takes place before the 7-year Tribulation that will happen once the Christians are removed. The Tribulation is a time when God pours out His wrath on a world that has rejected Jesus as their Savior. Believers are not appointed to suffer God's wrath, so we will be removed and taken into heaven for the duration of the Tribulation. At the conclusion of the Tribulation, we return with Jesus at His Second Coming and we will be reigning with Him on the earth.

The Rapture is described in 1 Thessalonians 4:16-17: *For the Lord himself will come down from heaven, with a loud command, with the voice of the archangel and with the trumpet call of God, and the dead in Christ will rise first. After that, we who are still alive and are left will be caught up together with them in the clouds to meet the Lord in the air. And so we will be with the Lord forever.* When it says that the "dead in Christ will rise first," it may prompt you to ask, "Where are the dead in Christ before the Rapture?" Their spirits are in heaven with Jesus, but their bodies are still in the ground. At the time of the Rapture, or the Resurrection, their bodies will be raised incorruptible – never to die again. After the dead are raised, the Christians who are truly Born Again (see John 3:3) will be changed to have the same glorious body as Christ. This is promised in Philippians 3:20-21: *But our citizenship is in heaven. And we eagerly await a Savior from there, the Lord Jesus Christ, who, by the power that enables him to bring everything under his control, will transform our lowly bodies so that they will be like his glorious body.* Another passage of Scripture that supports this position is 1 Corinthians 15:51-52: *Listen, I tell you a mystery: We will not all sleep, but we will all be changed – in a flash, in the twinkling of an eye, at the last trumpet. For the trumpet will sound, the dead will be raised imperishable, and we will be changed.*

If you knew the full extent of the horrors that will take place during the Tribulation period, then you would understand why it is better for you to receive Christ as your Savior now, for we do not know when Jesus is coming back. Because of the signs of the times, I believe that His return is very soon. It could happen at any moment. Are you ready to meet the soon coming King?

NOTES AND REFLECTIONS

NOTES AND REFLECTIONS

NOTES AND REFLECTIONS

CHAPTER 15

JESUS – SAVIOR OF THE WORLD

If the Lord has spoken to you through His Word recorded in this book, then I am pleased! But all your reading will be worth nothing unless you act upon what has been taught. This chapter will introduce you to Jesus as a Savior. He is the Savior of the world, and He is calling your name and inviting you into a relationship with Himself. Please note that I said a relationship, not a religion. There are many different religions and denominations out there, yet there is only one Lord. If you have not yet received Jesus into your heart, then I encourage you to prayerfully read this chapter with an open heart.

When God first created mankind, there was complete fellowship between man and God. Adam and Eve walked with God and enjoyed a beautiful relationship with Him. God gave them a beautiful place to live, called the Garden of Eden. They were free to enjoy each other and to enjoy God. God told them that they could eat from every tree in the garden, but they were not to eat the fruit from the tree of the Knowledge of Good and Evil. God told them that if they ate from that tree, they would surely die. Satan, who is the enemy of God, deceived Eve and she ate from that tree. She then gave some of the fruit to her husband and he ate, too. From this single act of disobedience, sin entered the world. As a result, every human being born on the face of the earth (except for Jesus) is guilty of sin. Romans 3:23 says, *"for all have sinned and fall short of the glory of God"*

The fellowship between God and mankind was broken, because God is Holy and sin cannot stand in His presence. Adam and Eve were expelled from the garden and, just as God said, they eventually experienced death. You may read of this account in Genesis chapter 3.

We were created to live forever. Every person has a soul that will go on living even after their body dies. Because of sin, we deserve eternal separation from God. This means that because we have violated God's righteous law, we can spend the rest of eternity in the Lake of Fire, created for the devil and his demons. This is not a place anyone would want to spend eternity (time without end). Those who reject Christ as their Savior will go to such a place. Eternity is a long time! God did not abandon us to our justly deserved fate, though. Because of His love for us, because of His infinite grace and mercy, He provided for our salvation through the Person of His Son, Jesus Christ! Please continue reading, as the following final point is very crucial and provides us with an everlasting hope!

God knew, before the world was ever created, that we would need a Savior. Jesus was ordained by His Father to be the sacrifice for our sins. Justice had to be met, and we were unable to meet God's standard of perfection. This is why it is important to understand that by merely being a good person, or doing a bunch of good deeds, does not fix the problem that sin has created. So God sent His son to earth, born of a virgin, and He lived a perfect life because He is God and was able to do so. Jesus was willing to pay our punishment and bear the wrath of God in our place on the cross. Jesus said in John 10:17-18, *"The reason my Father loves me is that I lay down my life – only to take it up again. No one takes it from me, but I lay it down of my own accord. I have authority to lay it down and authority to take it up again. This command I received from my Father."* Jesus died on the cross, shedding His precious blood for our salvation, and He died in our place. God laid on Jesus the sins of us all. This sacrifice pleased God and was acceptable to Him. Three days later, God raised Jesus from the dead and He is alive forever more! He is now in heaven, seated at the right hand of God. His Spirit lives on the inside of every believer who has put their faith in Jesus for salvation. If you choose to receive Jesus as your Savior, you will spend your eternity with Jesus, in complete wholeness and freedom and joy! Christ's life will be in you because the Holy Spirit will live on the inside of you. You will be free!

How Jesus longs to be your Savior! Please do not allow this moment to pass you by. This is your opportunity to receive forgiveness from your sins and allow Christ to take over. He is tenderly calling your name. If you would like to respond by inviting Jesus into your heart and life, then please pray the following prayer from your heart:

> *Dear Lord Jesus,*
>
> *I admit that I am a sinner. I believe that You died for my sins, shedding Your precious blood on the cross so that I may be forgiven. I also believe that God raised you to life on the third day. Please forgive me all my sins and come into my heart and life. I welcome you, Lord Jesus. Thank you for saving me!*
>
> *In Your Name I pray,*
>
> *Amen*

If you prayed that prayer sincerely from your heart, then welcome to the family of God! You are now a son or daughter of the Most High God, and you belong to Jesus. You may not necessarily "feel" any different now, but a tremendous difference has taken place. Once you were dead in your trespasses and sins; now you are alive in Christ! If you own a Bible, please read Romans chapter 8. I will write out verses 38-39 for you to encourage you: *For I am convinced that neither death nor life, neither angels nor demons, neither the present nor the future, nor any powers, neither height nor depth, nor anything else in all creation, will be able to separate us from the love of God that is in Christ Jesus our Lord.*

I encourage you to pray to your Heavenly Father, in Jesus' Name, often. I also encourage you to read your Bible daily because it is God's Word that is the standard for truth in our lives. It is His Word that heals us. If this is your first time reading the Bible, then I would suggest that you begin in the New Testament to have a firm foundation of grace. The Old Testament is just as important, but where you are a new student of God's Word, the New Testament will equip you for your journey ahead. I would also recommend that you pray for God to lead you to a church where Jesus is Lord and the Word of God is the focus. Bible study groups are also a great way to learn and grow. I lead a Bible study on Monday nights, as well as attend one that my Pastor facilitates on Wednesday nights. Knowing God's Word is crucial, especially given the times we are living in.

In this book, I have told you *about* Jesus. Now it is up to you to *know* Jesus by having a relationship with Him. Talk to Him often, for He is your closest friend. He will be everything you need to soar in this life. Then, when this life is over, you will have all eternity to spend in complete joy and fellowship with God. This will not be some boring future! Not at all. The future laid up for you as a child of God is filled with so much delight that I could not possibly explain it to you with words. In the book of Revelation, we see what God has in store for us after His return to earth. But you can enjoy the "good life" now, not just when you die. Christ lives on the inside of you, so you have a taste of heaven right here on earth. I will close this final chapter with Jesus' words in John 15:5: *I am the vine; you are the branches. If a man remains in me and I in him, he will bear much fruit; apart from me you can do nothing.*

NOTES AND REFLECTIONS

NOTES AND REFLECTIONS

NOTES AND REFLECTIONS

CONCLUSION

What a lovely name is Jesus! No other word is as sweet and no other person is as important as Christ. His heart is love and His gospel is worth dying for. It is not easy being a Christian. Jesus never promised that it would be. Many people resent God and take out their anger against Him on His followers. Satan, who is our enemy and desires to destroy us (see John 10:10), was defeated at the cross by Jesus. Christ is the One who is in control, and our truest treasure in heaven is Him!

I had wanted to make this book longer, for such a title warrants so much enthusiasm and detail. However, I decided that I would keep this simple, because the gospel is so simple that a child can grasp it! I was four years old when I heard the plan of salvation and invited Jesus into my heart. I am convinced that our salvation can never be taken away because, if it could, I would have lost mine years ago! I believe that just as we could not earn our salvation, neither can we maintain it. It is the grace of God and the sustaining power of Jesus Christ that ensures we are saved for all time. In John 10:27-30, Jesus says, *My sheep listen to my voice; I know them, and they follow me. I give them eternal life, and they shall never perish; no one can snatch them out of my hand. My Father, who has given them to me, is greater than all; no one can snatch them out of my Father's hand. I and the Father are one.*

I am now going to briefly share my testimony with you, because I am living proof that Jesus is all that the Word of God says He is. If you would like to read my testimony in detail, you may read my book, **From a Criminal Mind to the Mind of Christ**.

As previously mentioned, I accepted Jesus into my heart when I was four. But early on in life, it became very apparent that I had some deep emotional and mental health issues. By the time I was 22, I was in jail for a sentence of two-years-less-a-day. After my release, I became fascinated with crime and embraced it as a way of life. I lived in a fantasy world and became addicted to drugs. I seldom read the Bible or thought about Jesus. The extent of my prayer life was going to God when I was in big trouble, or to ask for His forgiveness periodically. Since the age of 16, I was admitted into psychiatric facilities on at least 5 or 6 occasions, possibly more. After my husband's death, I lost custody of my children, lost my home and became estranged from my family. I lived in a Second Stage Housing Project for a while, until I had a very real suicide attempt. I was then homeless, living in yet another psychiatric facility. It was then, through medication, prayer and God's Holy Word that I experienced healing. My family is now restored and I have enjoyed emotional and mental freedom for years. God used the "tragedies" in my life and turned them around for His glory. This same Jesus can do the same for you. All you have to do is ask Him.

Today, God has chosen to use me in various ministries through my church. My desire is to serve Jesus with all that I am and allow Him to work through me to reach as many people for the Lord as I can. I cannot take any credit for my success, because it was God who changed my focus and my will to be conformed to His will. 1 Corinthians 1:26-31 tells us, *Brothers, think of what you were when you were called. Not many of you were wise by human standards; not many were influential; not many were of noble birth. But God chose the foolish things of the world to shame the wise; God chose the weak things of the world to shame the strong. He chose the lowly things of this world and the despised things – and the things that are not – to nullify the things that are, so that no one may boast before him. It is because of him that you are in Christ Jesus, who has become for us wisdom from God – that is, our righteousness, holiness and redemption. Therefore, as it is written: "Let him who boasts boast in the Lord."*

Jesus Christ is the glory and the lifter of my head. When I am discouraged, He comforts me. When I am in despair, His Word gives me hope. When I feel the world closing in, He reminds me that I am His own. Who wouldn't want a Savior like this? He gives life and light to all those who call upon His Name. Drink from the fountain of living water that only Christ can give, and you will never be thirsty again! God bless you.

ABOUT THE AUTHOR

Melody Wolfe is a Christian author who is very passionate about the direction the Lord is taking her. She is blessed to have a wonderful family who supports her and love her. She is a proud mother of two daughters.

Melody is actively involved in ministry in her community. She leads a home group in her home on Sunday evenings, for people to come together to glorify the Lord. The Lord has given her a great desire to support her community, and she is dedicated to proclaiming the Gospel of Jesus Christ to any who is willing to listen. She is an active student of the Word of God and has a heart for those living with mental illness and addiction. Her prayer is that the Lord will reach those individuals who are actively involved in crime with His love, mercy and forgiveness.

Feel free to contact Melody at: melodywolfe@outlook.com.

This is now Melody's second book. Her first book was From a Criminal Mind to the Mind of Christ which received four out five stars on Amazon. com. It has been a long time before Melody found out she has the gift of writing and teaching. And she's so grateful she has these gifts to bring glory to the Lord.

Printed in the United States
By Bookmasters